INTERMEDIATE LEVEL

PEARL BUCK

The Good Earth

Retold by Stephen Colbourn

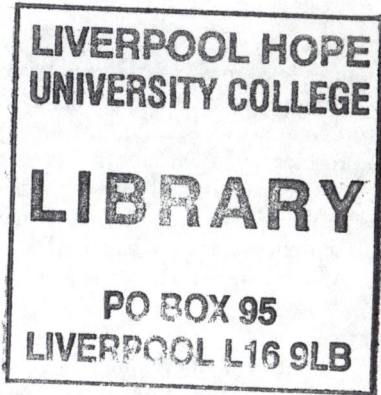

HEINEMANN

INTERMEDIATE LEVEL

Series Editor: John Milne

The Heinemann Guided Readers provide a choice of enjoyable reading material for learners of English. The Series is published at five levels – Starter, Beginner, Elementary, Intermediate and Upper. At **Intermediate Level**, the control of content and language has the following main features:

Information Control
Information which is vital to the understanding of the story is presented in an easily assimilated manner and is repeated when necessary. Difficult allusion and metaphor are avoided and cultural backgrounds are made explicit.

Structure Control
Most of the structures used in the Readers will be familiar to students who have completed an elementary course of English. Other grammatical features may occur, but their use is made clear through context and reinforcement. This ensures that the reading, as well as being enjoyable, provides a continual learning situation for the students. Sentences are limited in most cases to a maximum of three clauses and within sentences there is a balanced use of adverbial and adjectival phrases. Great care is taken with pronoun reference.

Vocabulary Control
There is a basic vocabulary of approximately 1600 words. Help is given to the students in the form of illustrations, which are closely related to the text.

Glossary
Some difficult words and phrases in this book are important for understanding the story. Some of these words are explained in the story, some are shown in the pictures, and others are marked with a number like this ... ³. Words with a number are explained in the Glossary on page 89.

Contents

A Note About the Author 5
A Note About China 7
The People in This Story 10

1 Wang Lung's Marriage Day 12
2 A Good Harvest 23
3 Wang Lung Buys Some Land 27
4 Wang Lung Leaves His Land 30
5 Begging in the City 34
6 When the Rich Are Too Rich ... 42
7 Another Visit to the House of Hwang 49
8 Cuckoo, Lotus and the Tea-house 54
9 Lotus Comes to Wang Lung's House 59
10 Wang Lung's Family 64
11 The Death of O-lan 72
12 War Comes to the North 79
13 The House of Wang Lung 81

Points for Understanding 85
Glossary 89
List of Titles at Intermediate Level 95

A Note About the Author

Pearl Sydenstricker Buck was born in 1892 in Hillsboro, West Virginia, USA. Her parents were both missionaries – religious teachers. When they went to work in China, they took Pearl and her brothers and sisters with them.

Pearl's parents travelled in China teaching the Christian religion. For a few years they lived in Chinkiang, on the Yangste River. When she was seventeen, Pearl was sent to Europe and then to America, to go to college.

After she had finished college in Virginia, USA, Pearl went back to China. Her mother was very ill at this time and Pearl looked after her. Pearl taught English literature at the University of Nanking and in the south-eastern University.

Her first book – *East Wind, West Wind* was published in 1929. *The Good Earth*, Pearl Buck's most famous novel, was published in 1931 and it was very successful. The story was made into a film in 1937, starring Paul Muni and Luise Rainer.

Pearl Buck won many prizes for her writing: the Pulitzer Prize (1931), the Howells Medal of the American Academy of Arts and Letters (1935) and the Nobel Prize for Literature (1938). She was married twice. Her first husband, Dr John Lossing Buck, worked as a missionary in Northern China. They had two daughters.

In 1934, Pearl Buck returned to America and lived in New York. She divorced John Buck and married Richard T. Walsh, a publisher, in 1935. Pearl and Richard went to live on a farm in Pennsylvania with their children. Pearl

Buck died in 1973.

Her best known books are: *East Wind, West Wind* (1929); *The Good Earth* (1931); *The Young Revolutionist* (1931); *Sons* (1932); *The First Wife and Other Stories* (1933); *The Mother* (1934); *A House Divided* (1935); *The Exile* (1936); *Fighting Angel* (1936); *The Patriot* (1937); *This Proud Heart* (1938); *The Chinese Novel* (1939); *Today and Forever* (1941); *Of Men and Women* (1941); *Dragon Seed* (1942); *American Unity and Asia* (1942).

A map of China showing the provinces.

A Note About China

China is a huge country (9597000 square km) which is divided into provinces. Today, these provinces are ruled by a central government in the capital, Beijing (Peking).

For more than 4000 years, China was ruled by powerful dynasties – or families – of emperors. Art, poetry, music, literature, architecture, philosophy, astronomy, medicine and mathematics were studied.

At the time of this story (1860–1930), the land belonged to rich landowners. But the work on the land was done by many millions of poor peasants. The peasants lived on the farms and had to pay rent to the landlords. Until 1911, when there was a revolution in China, the 459 million peasants had very little money and were un-educated. They had large families so that all the children could work on the land. There was very little machinery to help with the work, everything was done by the peasants and their animals. If the rains did not come, then the crops died, and often the peasants starved.

Family life was very important in China. Old relatives were respected and the younger people looked after them. Men were expected to marry by the time they were 30. Women were expected to marry by the time they were 20. A wife belonged to her husband.

While a father was alive his sons were under him. The oldest man was the head of the house.

Boys from rich families went to school from 10 to 15 years of age. Girls were not as important as boys. They did not go to school. They learnt how to look after the house. Fathers wanted sons who could work, earn money and look after them when they were old. Girls were often sold to be the slaves of rich landlords because the family could not pay the bride price for a marriage.

In the cities, rich people travelled by rickshaws – carts with two large wheels pulled by men – or they were carried in litters. A litter was a special seat on long poles that was carried by four or more men. Women often travelled in litters that had curtains all around them.

In the nineteenth century, the first railway trains were built in China. They travelled between the largest cities and ports. Also, at this time, bicycles started to be used in cities. But in the countryside, poor people walked everywhere or travelled on carts pulled by mules, horses or oxen.

For many years, the Chinese would not allow foreigners into their country. But soon people believed that China needed to understand and use new ideas from the west. In the story *The Good Earth*, Pearl Buck tells how the lives of the Chinese people began to change. In 1905, Sun Yatsen founded the Guomindang Political Party (GMD). Dr Sun had been educated by Europeans. He believed that European ideas and technology could make China very strong. In 1908, Empress Tzu-Hsi died. When the GMD took power in 1911, the Chinese dynasties were finished forever.

From 1911 to 1949 there was disorder and unrest in China. Armies from different groups fought with each other and with the Japanese. The Japanese saw that China was weak and in 1931 they entered the province of Manchuria in the north-east. The Japanese called Manchuria, Manchukuo. They made the young prince, Pu Yi, the Emperor of Manchukuo. But he only ruled for a very short time.

The People in This Story

Father

O-lan —m.— Wang Lung

Nung En   Nung Wen   Poor Fool

Great Lady of Hwang   Great Lord of Hwang   Ching

— Wang Lung's Uncle – *m.* – Wang Lung's Uncle's Wife

Wang Lung's Cousin.

the Twins

Lotus　　　　　Cuckoo　　　　Pear Blossom

11

1

Wang Lung's Marriage Day

Wang Lung woke up and tried to think why this day was different. The first light of dawn came in through the window of his small room. It was the light which woke him every morning, but today was different. Why? Then he remembered. Today, a woman was coming to the house. This was his marriage day.

Wang Lung's mother was dead. Wang Lung lived with his father in their small house made of earth. All the walls of the house were made of mud bricks and the roof was made of straw.

Wang Lung was a farmer. His father was a farmer – though he was now too old to work. His father's fathers had been farmers. It had always been so.

Wang Lung's old father coughed[1] in the next room. The old man coughed every morning until he drank a bowl of tea.

Wang Lung got up and went to heat water for his father's tea. He got some grass and dry leaves as fuel for the fire. Then he lit the fire on the mud bricks of the kitchen floor and put a pot of water over the fire.

'Tomorrow a woman will do this work,' he said to himself. 'Tomorrow my wife will do this work.'

Their earth house had three rooms. But now Wang Lung looked around the tiny kitchen and saw it was small. A woman was coming and, after she came, there would be children. Then they would build more rooms with mud bricks.

Wang Lung thought of all the beds they would need. He thought of the woman coming to the house and how she would help him with his work. Suddenly he thought of washing. He would wash all his body for the woman who was coming. And so he heated more water. And, because he was thinking about the woman, he forgot his father's tea.

His father came and stood in the kitchen doorway. The old man coughed.

'Why is there no water? Why must I cough and cough and have no water?'

'The fuel is wet and the pot is full,' replied Wang Lung. 'Soon the water will boil[2].'

He took a handful of tea-leaves from a jar and put them in a bowl. Then he poured boiling water from the pot onto the leaves.

The old man's eyes opened wide when he saw this. He began to complain[3], 'So many tea-leaves! Why so many? Why are you so wasteful today? Using so many tea-leaves is like drinking silver.'

'Today is my marriage day,' answered Wang Lung. 'Drink and be comforted[4].'

But the old man would not drink the tea. He watched the precious tea-leaves open up in the hot water and still he would not drink.

'The tea will be cold,' said Wang Lung.

'True – true.'

The old man suddenly began to drink the hot tea like a thirsty young child. He also watched as his son poured

'So many tea-leaves! Why so many?
Why are you so wasteful today?'

water into a bowl for washing.

'So much water! Why so much? That is enough water to grow a crop of rice.'

But Wang Lung poured all the hot water into the bowl and did not answer at once. He was too ashamed[5] to say, 'I wish my body to be clean for a woman to see.'

After a moment he spoke. 'I will throw the water on the earth and it will not be wasted.'

The old man was happy with this answer. He went to his room carrying his tea bowl. Wang Lung washed himself. Then he combed and braided[6] the long tail of hair that hung from the back of his head.

But the old man came to the kitchen again and said, 'Am I to have nothing to eat? It will be bad to show the woman that we live this way. Tea in the morning, and all this washing, and nothing to eat.'

'I will give you food,' answered Wang Lung, but he said to himself, 'That old man thinks of nothing but eating and drinking.'

He mixed a little ground corn[7] with hot water and gave it to his father.

'We will have rice tonight, my father. Meanwhile, here is corn.'

The old man stirred the yellow corn in the bowl with his chopsticks[8] then began to eat greedily.

'There is only a little rice. Do not waste it,' he said to his son.

'Yes, I know,' Wang Lung nodded his head and went to his own room. He took a leather pouch from a hole in the wall behind his bed. In the pouch was the money he had saved and hidden for his marriage day – six silver dollars and some copper pennies.

He had asked their relatives to eat with them that night, but he had not told his father. He was going to buy a little pork and fish, some water chestnuts and bamboo shoots[9], as well as soy-bean sauce[10] for the marriage feast. He must buy a stick of incense[11] to burn in the temple of the Earth God. Then the rains would come and water the earth, the crops would grow and they would have food to eat. He also wished to have his head shaved at the barber's shop.

He put on his best blue robe – the one that he wore on feast days – and picked up a basket made of bamboo. He left the house and walked across the green fields towards the grey town walls. There, in the town, lived the woman in the House of Hwang – a slave woman in the great House of Hwang.

His father had arranged the marriage. The old man had gone to the House of Hwang and asked if there was a slave woman he could buy.

'I don't want a young slave or a pretty slave,' he had said. 'But a slave for a poor man – one who will tend the house and work the fields and bear children[12].'

Wang Lung had said to his father, 'Don't get a woman who is pock-marked[13], or who has a split upper lip[14].' And his father had agreed to this. Then he had bought marriage gifts – two silver rings covered with gold, and two ear-rings also of silver.

Now Wang Lung stood alone in the Street of the Barbers and did not know what to do or say. He did not often come into town and he had never spoken to a barber. He walked along the whole street, looking at all the barbers' stalls. Then he sat down in the chair at the last stall.

'Shall I shave everything?' asked the barber.

'My head and my face,' replied Wang Lung.

'Do you want your ears and nostrils cleaned?'

'How much extra will that cost?' Wang Lung asked.

'Four pence,' answered the barber.

'I will give you two pence,' said Wang Lung.

'Then I will clean one ear and one nostril,' the barber said and laughed loudly. The barbers in the other stalls nearby all laughed at Wang Lung, the simple farmer.

'All right – I will pay four pence,' Wang Lung said quickly and paid the money. It was such a lot of money. But the town barbers had made him feel a fool. And he wished to hide his ignorance[15].

'This simple farmer could be good-looking without his braid of hair,' the barber said loudly. 'It is now the fashion to cut it off.' And the barber's sharp razor moved towards Wang Lung's braid.

'Don't cut my braid!' said Wang Lung angrily. He left as soon as the barber had finished shaving the rest of his head.

From the Street of the Barbers, Wang Lung went to the market. Here he counted his money carefully. Then he bought two pounds of pork and six ounces of beef and several squares of bean-curd[16]. All these were wrapped in lotus leaves and placed carefully in his basket. After that, he bought two sticks of incense. Then he was ready to meet his bride[17].

He walked slowly to the great House of Hwang and stood in front of the huge gates. He was afraid. The house was so big. How many people lived here? Dozens? Hundreds? Two stone lions guarded[18] the gates which were made of wood and iron. He had never been inside a house with walls and gates like these. He stood staring at the house.

'Now then, what do you want?' demanded[19] the gate-keeper. He was a tall, rough man who was cleaning his teeth with a bamboo stick. The gatekeeper was polite only to the rich friends of his master and Wang Lung looked like a beggar.

'I ... I am Wang Lung ... the farmer.'

'Yes, Wang Lung the farmer, what do you want?'

'I am come ... I am come ...'

'Yes, yes, I can see that,' said the gatekeeper. He looked at Wang Lung's basket. 'Have you come to sell something?'

'There is ... a woman ...'

'A woman!' The gatekeeper laughed loudly. 'Ah – you are the bridegroom! Yes, yes, Wang Lung the farmer, you are expected[20].' Then he stood waiting.

'Am I to go in alone?' asked Wang Lung.

'The old Lord will kill you if you do,' said the gate-keeper.

'But, I am expected.'

The gatekeeper saw that Wang Lung was an ignorant farmer and said, 'A little silver is a good key to open these gates. Have you any money?'

'I have a few copper pennies and a silver dollar.'

'I will take the silver dollar,' said the gatekeeper and held out his hand.

Wang Lung was ashamed and angry, but he gave his last silver dollar to the gatekeeper. Then the gatekeeper led him into the great house past the stone lions.

'The bridegroom! The bridegroom!' the gatekeeper shouted.

Wang Lung followed him. The young man bowed his head down in anger and shame as they walked through a dozen courtyards[21] of the great house.

'Put down your basket before you see the Great Lady,' the gatekeeper said to Wang Lung.

'But ... but ... someone may take it,' Wang Lung replied.

'We feed our dogs with better food than you have in your basket,' said the gatekeeper. 'Now, remember. When I bring you to the Great Lady, you must fall on your face.' Then he led Wang Lung into a hall with a high ceiling.

Wang Lung had never seen a room like this. The ceiling of the hall was made with carved and painted beams. The hall was as big as twenty houses. And in the centre of the hall sat the Great Lady of the House of Hwang.

She was a very old lady. Her small, thin body was clothed in pearly grey silk and on a low bench beside her stood a pipe of opium[22]. She looked at Wang Lung with her small, sharp, black eyes. Her face was like a monkey's face.

Wang Lung fell on his face in front of her and put his forehead on the tiled floor.

'Make him stand,' the old lady commanded[23] the gatekeeper. 'Has he come for the slave woman?'

'Yes, Ancient One,' replied the gatekeeper.

19

'Send for her quickly,' commanded the old lady and then her hand closed on the opium pipe and raised it to her mouth. She sucked quickly on the pipe like a thirsty child. Her eyes lost their sharpness and she forgot why Wang Lung was there.

'Why is this man here?' she asked suddenly, staring at Wang Lung.

'He has come for the slave woman, O-lan,' answered the gatekeeper.

'Call O-lan, quickly,' commanded the old lady.

And O-lan came and stood in front of the Great Lady. She stood with her head bowed and looked at the ground. O-lan was wearing a blue cotton coat and trousers. Her hair was neat and smooth and clean.

Wang Lung looked quickly at his bride and was pleased with what he saw. She was not pretty. She looked like a farmer's wife. This was good.

'Are you ready to go with this man?' asked the Great Lady.

'Yes ... I am ready,' answered O-lan slowly.

Wang Lung heard her voice. It was a good voice, though she spoke slowly.

'Obey[24] this man, your husband,' commanded the Great Lady. 'Bear him sons and more sons. Bring the first child for me to see.'

'Yes, Ancient Mistress,' said O-lan.

'Now, carry her box to the gate,' commanded the Great Lady. 'Let them be gone.'

The gatekeeper carried O-lan's box to the gates and Wang Lung and O-lan followed. When they got to the big

'Why is this man here?' she asked suddenly,
staring at Wang Lung.

gates, Wang Lung took the box, which contained his wife's few possessions[25]. Then he stood in front of the woman and looked at her.

She had a square honest face, a short broad nose with large black nostrils and her mouth was wide. Her eyes were small and full of sadness. It was the face of a silent woman who had borne many hardships[26] and would bear more. And in her ears were the two rings of silver which Wang Lung had given her, and on her fingers were the two rings of silver covered with gold. And so, Wang Lung and O-lan were man and wife and O-lan came to live in the small house of Wang Lung and his father.

That night, Wang Lung's uncle and his uncle's son came to the marriage feast. O-lan cooked the food, but she did not eat with the men. She stayed in the kitchen.

'I will give you the bowls of food,' O-lan said to her husband. 'I do not like to come out of the kitchen when there are men visiting the house.'

Wang Lung was pleased that she said this and so was his father. Wang Lung's uncle understood that O-lan was a modest[27] woman and he spoke well of the food and her cooking.

'It is a simple meal. It is badly prepared,' said Wang Lung quickly. But in his heart, he was pleased by his uncle's words and with O-lan. And that night, when the guests had left and the meal had been cleared away, he took O-lan to his bed.

2

A Good Harvest

In the next few weeks, O-lan showed that she could tend the house. She cleaned and cooked and mended clothes and fed the ox[28] which they kept behind the kitchen. And in the afternoons O-lan came out into the field and worked silently beside her husband.

The two of them worked together. They hoed[29] the earth and planted seed and reaped[30] the crops from the land.

One evening, as the sun was setting, O-lan stopped working and spoke quietly to Wang Lung.

'I am going to have a child.'

Wang Lung stopped hoeing and looked at her with pleasure[31]. He took the hoe from her hand. Then he led her home to where his old father stood on the doorstep waiting impatiently for his supper.

'I am too old to wait for my food,' he complained.

Wang Lung said to his father, 'She is going to have a child.'

And his old father looked at O-lan. 'He-he-he,' laughed the old man, 'so we will have a good harvest this year[32].'

'I shall prepare food now,' said O-lan.

'Oh. Yes, yes – food,' said the old man happily. And he followed her into the kitchen like a child. The thought of a grandson had made him forget his meal. Now the thought of food made him forget the child.

Wang Lung sat on a bench by a table in the darkness

and folded his arms. He put his head on his arms which were the colour of the brown earth. And he thought how this new life had come out of his body.

———

When the hour for the birth of their child was near, Wang Lung spoke to his wife. 'You must have some help with this thing – a woman from the village must come to help you with the birth.'

But O-lan shook her head and cleared away the bowls from their evening meal silently.

Wang Lung was worried. 'Perhaps we can ask a woman from the great House of Hwang to help with this thing – a woman who worked with you.'

Then O-lan turned to her husband angrily. 'I want no one from that house,' she said bitterly.

Wang Lung was surprised because his wife had never spoken to him like that before.

'When I return to that house,' O-lan continued, 'it will be with my son in my arms. He shall wear a red coat. I shall go into the great hall, where the Old One sits with her opium, and I shall show myself and my son.'

'I suppose you will need money for a red coat,' said Wang Lung.

'If you will give me three silver dollars – I know it is a great amount of money – I will not waste a penny of it.'

So Wang Lung gave her the money and thought about the silver dollars. It had come out of the earth, this silver. Every mouthful of food, every copper penny and silver dollar, came out of the earth which he ploughed[33] and planted and reaped. Before he was married, each time he had spent a silver dollar, it was like giving away a piece of his own life. But, now, for the first time, it was not hard to spend money. The silver was for his son.

Wang Lung and O-lan worked in the field all the next day. O-lan bent over slowly because of her swollen belly. Then suddenly, she stopped, stood up and dropped her hoe. There was the sweat[34] of pain on her face.

'It is time,' she said. 'I will go to the house. Do not come into the room until I call. Then bring me a freshly peeled reed[35] so that I may cut the child's life from mine.'

Wang Lung went to the pond and cut a reed. Then he walked home slowly. His father was in the kitchen eating his supper.

'The child is coming, but it will be a long time,' said the old man. 'I remember when my first child was born. And after that – how many? I forget. The first one took the longest to be born. You were my last child and only you have lived.'

Wang Lung went to the bedroom door. 'Here is the reed,' he said.

O-lan opened the door a little but she did not let Wang Lung come in. She put her hand round the door and took the peeled reed. Then she shut the door again. Wang Lung waited and listened. He heard his wife breathing like an animal. A smell of hot blood came from the room – a smell that frightened him. And, at last, he heard a thin, fierce cry.

'Is it a man?' he called to his wife, forgetting the woman's pain.

The voice of the woman answered quietly, 'It is a man.'

Wang Lung went to the pond and cut a reed.
Then he walked home slowly.

Wang Lung entered the room. The child was wrapped in a pair of old trousers. It had a round, small face and on its head the hair was wet and black.

He looked at his wife. Her hair was wet with the sweat of her pain. He smiled at the mother and child.

'We shall buy a basket of eggs and paint them red. I shall take them to the village. Then everyone will know I have a son!'

3

Wang Lung Buys Some Land

O-lan returned to work in the fields a few days after the baby was born. She brought the small child with her and laid him on an old quilt[36] by the pond. When she rested from her work, she lifted the child to her breast and let him feed.

Summer passed and Wang Lung and O-lan prepared for winter. They salted[37] meat and hung vegetables from the ceiling of their house and put their corn in baskets. There was more food than they needed so they would sell the extra food.

Wang Lung waited until the New Year before he sold his corn. At that time, when snow was on the ground, prices were high and he earned a large amount of silver. This was more money than he had ever had and he was worried that it might be stolen. O-lan hid the silver in a hole in the wall behind their bed. The silver was their secret treasure and comfort[38].

On the second day of the New Year, O-lan dressed her child in a new red coat which she had made. She had also made new black coats for herself and her husband. It was time to show the child to the Great Lady at the House of Hwang. And it was time to show that she, who was once a slave girl in that house, had prospered[39].

The gatekeeper of the House of Hwang stared at Wang Lung and his family. He saw their new clothes and he also saw that their child was a son, which was a sign of good fortune[40].

'Wang Lung, the farmer,' said the gatekeeper. 'You have had good fortune. There is no need to wish you more good fortune this year.' He no longer talked to Wang Lung as if he was a beggar.

'We had a good harvest,' said Wang Lung, as if it were a small thing.

Then Wang Lung sat and waited while the gatekeeper showed O-lan into the house. The gatekeeper's wife brought tea to Wang Lung. He did not drink it, but he was pleased that she brought it.

After a time O-lan came back, holding the child. Wang Lung looked closely at his wife's face and saw that she, too, was pleased. He wanted to ask her about the Great Lady and what she had said. But he waited until they had left the gatekeeper and his wife.

'No one in the House of Hwang has a new coat this year,' said O-lan as they walked home. 'The Ancient One said that they need to sell land.'

'Then, indeed, they are becoming poor,' said Wang

'Wang Lung, the farmer,' said the gatekeeper.
'You have had good fortune.'

Lung. And suddenly he cried out, 'I have decided! We have silver. We will buy land from the House of Hwang!'

Wang Lung took his silver from the hole in the wall of the mud house. And next day, at noon, he returned to the House of Hwang.

'Tell His Honour I have important business,' Wang Lung said to the gatekeeper.

'I dare not[41] wake the Old Lord,' the gatekeeper replied. 'He sleeps with his new concubine, Peach Blossom.'

And so Wang Lung had to speak with the Old Lord's agent who looked after all the business of the House of Hwang. This oily[42] man looked at Wang Lung's silver and said, 'This will buy a few days of opium for the Great Lady.'

And the money bought Wang Lung a field of land near to the House of Hwang on the edge of the town. The land was Wang Lung's, but he was angry that his silver would be wasted on opium. He said to himself, 'I will work to fill the hole in my wall with silver again.'

4

Wang Lung Leaves His Land

Wang Lung was now a landowner and a prosperous man, but he did not speak of his good fortune. He feared that the gods or his fellow men would envy[43] him. Also O-lan gave birth to a second son and was soon with child again for the third time. The villagers saw Wang Lung's prosperity and talked of making him Head Man.

But then his fortune changed. The next summer no rain fell. The fields became dry and cracked and only a few poor shoots of corn grew in them. Even the pond and the well were almost dry.

'The children and the old man must have water to drink,' said O-lan. 'Save the water in the well. Do not put it on the dry fields.'

'If the plants do not get water and grow, we will all starve,' answered Wang Lung.

And before winter, O-lan gave birth to another child. This time it was a girl. 'A slave,' said O-lan. 'A girl child. A little fool.' And so there was another mouth to feed in Wang Lung's house.

Still no rains came and the villagers grew desperate. They were hungry, angry and afraid. They said to each other that Wang Lung had hidden silver and food. But if they had asked him, 'What will you and your family eat this winter?' Wang Lung would have replied, 'I do not know.'

At the end of the year, the villagers came to Wang Lung's house. They were desperate with hunger. They beat upon the door with wooden sticks and then pushed their way inside.

'Where is the food?' they cried.

They pushed Wang Lung and his family outside, then they searched the house. The only food they found was a bowl of corn and a handful of beans, so they started to pull the furniture out of the house.

'Leave the table and benches!' cried O-lan. 'Have you sold your own tables and benches? You have more food than us because now we have none. At least leave us our few pieces of furniture.'

Then the villagers were ashamed and left the house. They were not evil men, except when they were desperate with hunger.

So Wang Lung was left in his house with his crying children, his frightened father and his trembling[44] wife. There was no food now. The villagers had taken it all.

'They would have taken the silver,' thought Wang Lung. 'But I have none. I used all the silver to buy land. They cannot take the land from me.'

But Wang Lung and his family could not stay on the land. If they stayed they would starve. 'We must go south,' he said. 'There is always food in the south where it is warm. We will take only the things we can carry. I will sell the furniture and leave the house empty.'

'But do not sell the tools,' said O-lan. 'We will need the tools to work on the land when we return.'

So Wang Lung went to a merchant in the town and sold all his furniture. The merchant took away the beds and benches and table and paid two silver dollars.

'It is not much money. It is the price of half a bed,' said O-lan.

Then they shut the door of the empty house and they started to walk south. Their only possessions were the clothes they were wearing and their rice bowls and chopsticks.

O-lan gave her bowl and chopsticks to the two boys so

that she could carry the tiny girl. Her daughter was a few months old and thin and ill.

Wang Lung helped his old father to walk. He was weak, but his old father weighed almost nothing.

'There is warmth in the south and rice,' he said to the boys. 'In the south you can eat and eat.'

They walked through the town slowly and came near to the House of Hwang. The gates were shut and locked and a few beggars lay in front of them. One beggar cried out, 'They have rice to eat while we starve! A thousand curses[45] on the House of Hwang!'

When Wang Lung and his family had passed through the town and come out on the other side, they saw a large crowd of people. Wang Lung asked a man, 'Where are all these people going?'

The man answered, 'They are going to get on the fire wagons and ride to the south. You may ride on the fire wagons for a few pence.'

'I have heard of these wagons which run on an iron road,' said Wang Lung, 'though I have never seen them.' And he asked O-lan, 'Shall we ride on these fire wagons?'

O-lan said nothing. The old man and the boys sat down on the ground. The baby girl lay silently in her mother's arms. There was a look of death on the child's face.

'Does the little slave still live?' asked Wang Lung.

'There is still breath in her body,' answered O-lan, 'but she will die this night.'

They would not have moved from there, except that a sound came out of the darkness. Suddenly, with the noise of a dragon, the fire wagons came along on their road of iron. The people around the family began to shout and push. Wang Lung's family held each other and tried to keep together. Then the crowd ran towards the boxes of the fire wagons and Wang Lung and his family were pushed inside.

5

Begging in the City

There was no time to think about this strange way of travelling. An official collected money from the crowd. Wang Lung's two silver dollars paid for the family to travel a hundred miles of iron road. He now had a few copper pennies left.

A food-seller pushed his way into the wagon. Wang Lung bought four small loaves of bread and a bowl of rice. This was more food than the Wang family had eaten for days and the boys could not swallow it easily. The old man sucked on his bread, laughed and said, 'My foolish belly has grown lazy from little work. It is not used to food.'

There were men and women in the fire wagon who knew the cities of the south.

'How can we live in the south?' Wang Lung asked.

'You must buy six mats,' said one man. 'They cost two pence each.'

'And then?' asked Wang Lung.

'Then ...' said the man, '... you join the mats together to

34

Wang Lung's family held each other
and tried to keep together.

make a hut in which to live. And then you go out to beg for money in the streets.'

'Must we beg?' asked Wang Lung in surprise.

'Yes,' replied the man, 'but only after you have eaten. There are public kitchens[46] where you may eat if you pay a penny. When your belly is full, you can beg for money to buy bean-curd, cabbage and garlic.'

Wang Lung stood away from the others. He had never begged and he did not like the idea. Secretly, he counted his few pence. There was enough money to buy mats.

The fire wagon stopped next morning and they all got out. They stared around them at the people of the south. They had pale, oily skins and spoke strangely. Wang Lung could not easily understand what these southern people were saying.

He told O-lan to wait with his father and the children by a long grey wall. Then he went to find a shop which sold mats. He knew the price was two pence a mat.

When he returned, carrying the mats, there were already new huts beside the long grey wall. The wall gave shelter from the cold wind. No one knew what was on the other side of the wall and no one cared.

'Give the mats to me,' said O-lan. 'I learnt how to join them together when I was a child.'

She made a simple hut, like the other huts against the wall. Each hut was so close to the next one that Wang Lung could reach out and touch his neighbours' huts.

Wang Lung found the public kitchens, which were for the poor people of the city. Huge pots of rice were stood on fires. These pots were as big as small ponds and many men

36

and women crowded round to get the food. He stood with the crowd, paid his penny and held out his rice bowl. The bowl was filled. He could not understand why people were doing this for him.

A guard, dressed in a blue and red uniform, stood near the door to the kitchen. Wang Lung asked him, 'How can so many men be fed for a penny? Who gives away this rice?'

And the guard answered, 'The rich men of the city give this rice.'

'But why?' asked Wang Lung. 'Why does any man give food to the poor like this?'

'Some men do it as a good deed,' answered the guard, 'so that by saving lives they may get merit in heaven[47]. And some men do it so that their fellow men will speak well of them.'

'And some men do good things because they have good hearts,' said Wang Lung. But the guard did not reply.

The next morning, Wang Lung and his family needed more money. O-lan had the answer.

'I and the children and the old man will beg in the street,' she said. 'We will hold our rice bowls in our hands and call out, 'Do you have a good heart, sir? Do you have a good heart, kind lady? A good deed will surely get merit in heaven. Give a penny. Feed a starving child.'

Wang Lung stared at her. 'Where did you learn this?' he asked. 'Where did you learn to beg in the street?'

'I learnt this when I was a child,' answered O-lan. 'I learnt to beg one year when there was no food. In that year, I was sold as a slave to the House of Hwang.'

The old man, who had been sleeping, awoke. O-lan put a bowl into his hand and also bowls into the hands of the two boys. Then they went out into the street and began to beg.

O-lan held the tiny girl to her breast. The child slept, but her head hung over to one side as though she were dead.

'We starve!' O-lan called out. 'Give a penny, or the child will die!'

The two boys played at begging. They had forgotten their hunger already. Begging was a game to them. They called out – 'We starve! We starve!' – then they laughed with embarrassment[48]. When she heard them, O-lan became angry and beat the boys.

'Do you talk of starving and laugh at the same time? You fools! You will certainly starve!' And she beat them again and again until her hand hurt and the tears ran down the boys' faces.

'Now you can beg,' said O-lan.

Wang Lung was ashamed that his family had become beggars. He went to look for work and found a place where rickshaws were hired[49]. The owner of all the rickshaws explained the business to Wang Lung.

'You can take one of my rickshaws to carry passengers,' he said. 'Ask for as much money as the passengers will pay. Every night, you will give me half a silver dollar. You can keep the rest of the money for yourself.'

Wang Lung took the rickshaw and went out into the street. The work was harder than the work in the fields. He was used to digging with a hoe, not pulling a rick-

'We starve!' O-lan called out. 'Give a penny,
or the child will die!'

shaw. At first he did not know how to find the places the passengers wanted to go to. He did not know how much money to ask for. But he learnt quickly. However, that night, after he had paid half a silver dollar to the rickshaw owner, there was only one copper penny left for himself.

Wang Lung went back to the hut and found that O-lan had been given forty small coins for her day's begging. These were worth four copper pennies. The older boy had eight small coins and the younger boy had thirteen.

The old man had not been given any money. He had slept beside the road and had not begged. 'I have ploughed land and planted seed and filled my rice bowl,' he said. 'And I have made sons.' He believed that his family would feed him.

As Wang Lung lay down after his day of work, he thought about his land. It was waiting for him, far to the north, and the thought filled him with peace.

―――

The days passed, and Wang Lung pulled the rickshaw through the streets of the great city of the south. He saw many new and strange things. The farmers in this land spread stinking manure[50] on the earth. And the crops grew well. Everywhere there was food. He saw rice and corn. Fish, still alive, moved in baskets in the fish market. Huge pieces of meat hung in the butcher's shops.

But Wang Lung could not earn enough money so his family went to the public kitchen for food. If there was an extra penny or two, O-lan cooked rice and cabbage in their hut. She had found two bricks and an old metal pot that someone had thrown away. But fuel for the fire was hard to find. The boys stole reeds or hay from the farmers' carts and the farmers chased them away. The older boy was big and slow but the younger one was quick and clever and could always find some sticks or dry grass for fuel.

One night, Wang Lung came home to find O-lan cooking a large piece of pork.

'Who gave us this meat?' asked Wang Lung.

'I took it when the butcher wasn't looking,' the younger boy answered, 'It is mine!'

When he heard this Wang Lung was very angry. 'I will not eat this meat!' he shouted. 'We will only eat meat that we can buy or beg for. We will not eat meat that we steal!'

'Meat is meat,' said O-lan quietly.

She took the cooked meat and broke it apart with her chopsticks. She gave some to the old man and the boys and filled the young girl's mouth with it as well as her own. But Wang Lung would not eat any of it. He took the young boy out of the hut and beat him, saying, 'Take that for being a thief!' And he beat him again.

The boy ran back to his mother, crying bitterly. Wang Lung stood alone outside the hut in the night.

'We must get back to our land,' he said.

6

When the Rich Are Too Rich …

Months passed and Wang Lung and his family did not return to their land. They were still poor but they knew where they could get food in the city. Wang Lung heard no news from his village and he did not know if it was safe to return.

It was such a long way back to his own land. Could the old man and the children walk all that way? And what if they found at the end of their journey that nothing had changed?

'If only I could earn a little more money,' he thought. 'When we return, we will need to buy seed to plant in the earth. And how will we live until the seed has grown?' And he thought of the secret hole in the wall of the house where he had kept his silver. Now they could earn only enough to feed themselves and there was nothing left over. Would he ever have more silver to put in his secret place?

Wang Lung now understood that most people in this great city were poor. They could not save any money. These poor people worked all the time but they had little money and few possessions. A few people did not work – they were idle – but they were rich. They had money and jewels and fine houses.

'If I had anything to sell, I would sell it and return to our land,' he said to O-lan.

'There is the girl,' said O-lan. 'We can sell her as a

slave. I was sold as a slave to the House of Hwang.'

The little girl had grown stronger and was learning to walk. She looked at her father and smiled. Wang Lung's heart was full of love for her. He remembered that when she was born she had nearly starved to death.

'I cannot sell her,' said Wang Lung. 'She has such a sweet smile that I cannot do it.'

Then Wang Lung stood outside his hut and said loudly, 'Will I never see my land again?'

His neighbour spoke to him from the doorway of the next hut, 'There are hundreds of poor people like us in this city.'

'Will our lives always be like this?' asked Wang Lung.

'No,' answered the man. 'When the rich are too rich and the poor are too poor, things always change.'

'I know little about the lives of rich men,' said Wang Lung.

'And they know little about your life,' his neighbour said and laughed. 'But only a wall keeps us apart.'

'What do you mean?' asked Wang Lung. He thought that the neighbour meant the walls of their huts. The walls of mats were so thin that people heard everything that happened in their neighbours' huts.

The neighbour pointed behind them at the long grey wall. 'This is the wall of a great house,' he said. 'The rich people inside throw away more possessions in one day than you will ever own in a lifetime. They have pearls and gold and silver. Their dogs eat better food than you do. The rich are too rich but there is a way we can change this.'

That night, Wang Lung dreamt of silver. But he did not think of what his neighbour meant when he said, 'The rich are too rich but there is a way we can change this.'

———

In the spring, Wang Lung often saw groups of men standing in the streets listening to someone speaking. Then other men came and gave out leaflets to the people who were listening.

One day, as he was pulling the rickshaw, Wang Lung stopped near a group of these men. He heard a young speaker say, 'The rich oppress[51] the poor. The rich make us poor.'

Wang Lung had always thought he was poor because the gods did not make enough rain for the crops to grow well. So he went up to the speaker and asked, 'Sir, is there any way that the rich, who oppress us, can make it rain?'

'You are ignorant,' said the young man. 'You still wear your hair in a long braid. The rich cannot make it rain. But if they shared the food and wealth with us, then rain would not matter.'

There was a great shout from the crowd and a man pushed some leaflets into Wang Lung's hand. These leaflets meant nothing to Wang Lung because he could not read or write. But he took them, remembering that O-lan wanted paper to burn on the fire and to put in their thin shoes.

Wang Lung did not agree with the young man's words. Food is soon eaten and money is soon gone. But if there is not sun and rain, then the land will not grow crops and hunger will come.

Suddenly there was shouting and soldiers appeared in the streets. They had guns and knives and caught several men from the group. All the other men ran away. But Wang Lung could not run away and leave the rickshaw, so he hid in an old man's shop.

'Lie on the floor,' said the old man, 'the soldiers will soon be gone.'

'What are they doing?' asked Wang Lung.

'They are taking men to fight in the war,' the old man answered.

'Do they take men from their families?' asked Wang Lung in horror. He thought of wives and children left to starve when their men were taken to die in battle.

'The soldiers do not care about the mens' families,' said the old man. 'Now, the soldiers are gone. Hurry home quickly.'

Wang Lung ran home with the rickshaw as fast as he could. He told O-lan what he had seen. 'We must go back to our land,' he said.

'Wait a few days,' said O-lan. 'I have heard news. The neighbours say there is going to be a battle.'

Next day, Wang Lung did not leave the hut because he feared the soldiers. He sent the oldest boy to return the rickshaw to its owner.

Two days later the public kitchen closed. Then Wang Lung left his hut and spoke to the guard outside the kitchen.

'Why has the kitchen closed?'

'The rich men of the city, who pay for the kitchen, are leaving,' answered the guard. 'They want to take all their money with them. But it is too late. The gates of the city are closed. The enemy is outside the city. No one may enter or leave.'

Wang Lung returned to his hut. On the way, he saw that the streets were empty. Everyone who owned anything was afraid because the enemy was close. But the poor people who lived in the huts by the wall of the great house were not afraid because they had nothing to lose. They sat in their huts and waited. Wang Lung did not know who the enemy was. But he feared the soldiers and stayed in his hut because he did not know what to do.

'We must escape from this city,' he said. 'There is no work and no food. If we stay here, we will starve.'

And he took his small daughter in his arms and said, 'Little fool, would you like to go to the great house behind the wall? There is food and drink in the great house.'

His daughter smiled, not understanding what he said. Then Wang Lung spoke to O-lan, 'Were you often beaten in the House of Hwang?'

And O-lan answered, 'Every day I was beaten.'

Suddenly there was a great roaring and crashing sound. Wang Lung and his family all fell onto the ground and hid their faces. Wang Lung covered the girl child's face with his hand and the two boys shouted in fear. Then they heard a great noise, as though many men cried out in the city with one voice.

'The enemy has broken down the gates of the city,' said O-lan.

And then another sound, much nearer, came to them. They heard the creaking of a large door.

'Come, the doors of the rich man's house are open,' called their neighbour.

O-lan moved quickly and left the hut. Wang Lung said to the old man and the children, 'Stay here.' Then he went and followed O-lan.

Many men were running towards the doors of the great house. They made noises in their throats like tigers. Wang Lung went with them and was pushed inside the great house. The crowd ran through the house, searching rooms, opening boxes, pulling at curtains, taking dishes and clothes.

Wang Lung came to the inner courtyard[52] where the ladies of the rich lived. He saw the small door at the back of the great house, which is called the gate of peace. The women of the inner courtyard had escaped through this door.

One man had not escaped. This fat man came out of an inner room. His face was fat and his eyes were small like pig's eyes. He seemed half-asleep or drunk. When he saw Wang Lung he cried out, 'Save a life – save a life – do not kill me! I have money for you – much money.'

Wang Lung had no weapon and he did not attack the man. But the word 'money' lit a fire in his head. Money! The girl-child would be saved. He could go back to his land! And he shouted in a rough voice, 'Give me the money!'

The man took a handful of gold from the pocket of his robe and held it out to Wang Lung.

'Give me more!' shouted Wang Lung.

And again the man put his hand into his pocket and

The man took a handful of gold from the pocket of his robe
and held it out to Wang Lung.

took out more money. 'Now there is nothing left and I have nothing but my life to lose,' he said. And he began to cry.

'Go now, or I will kill you,' shouted Wang Lung.

The man ran out of the gate of peace and was gone.

Wang Lung was left alone with two handfuls of gold. He hid the money inside his shirt and returned to his hut.

7

Another Visit to the House of Hwang

Next day, everyone was moving around in the city. No one was working. Crowds of people moved towards the city gates and no one stopped them leaving.

'We will go north,' Wang Lung said to his family. 'We will return to the land which is ours.'

And so they began the long walk back to their own land.

It was a long journey, but the weather was good and the road was peaceful. The war was far away in the south of the country. Wang Lung and his family bought food on the way, for now they had money.

At last, Wang Lung reached his land in the north. Their house, made of earth, was still there, but the door and the roof were gone. Wang Lung was not worried because now he had money to buy a new door, a new roof, new furniture and new tools to work on the land.

He went to his neighbour's house and asked, 'Ching,

who took the door and the roof from my house?'

And Ching answered, 'Bandits[53] lived in your house last winter. Your uncle saw them. They built a fire from your wooden door and straw roof.'

'And how did you live through the time of hunger?' asked Wang Lung.

'We ate dogs. We ate grass. Some people even ate the flesh of the dead. My wife died and I gave my daughter to a soldier. Now I am alone.'

Then Wang Lung said, 'I have seed. I have land. Come and work on my land and you shall eat.'

So the neighbour, Ching, came to work for Wang Lung. Other men came to work for him also, but Ching was Wang Lung's first workman. So Ching was put in charge of the workmen – he was their foreman.

———

One night, after the house had been repaired, Wang Lung lay with his wife. He felt a lump between her breasts.

'What is this thing?' he asked.

O-lan showed him a small leather pouch that was tied on a cord around her neck. 'I took this from the great house in the city of the south,' she said.

There were jewels inside the bag – red and green and white stones – the treasure of a rich man. Wang Lung held wealth[54] in his hands.

'Treasure like this must be sold,' he said. 'It is not safe to keep it. We must buy land.'

'I wish I could keep two stones for myself,' said O-lan sadly. 'Only two small ones. Perhaps the two white pearls?'

'What for?' asked Wang Lung in surprise. 'Why do you

'Treasure like this must be sold,' he said.
'It is not safe to keep it.'

need pearls?'

'I would not wear them,' answered O-lan. 'I would keep them. Perhaps, sometimes, I would hold them in my hands. And when our daughter marries, I will give them to her to make into earrings.'

Then Wang Lung looked at his good wife who had worked for many years. He saw she wanted something for herself and he gave her the two pearls. She took them and hid them in the pouch around her neck and she was comforted.

Next day, Wang Lung went to the House of Hwang to see if they wished to sell more land. There was no gate-keeper and the gates were closed. He knocked on the gates, but there was no answer.

A man passing by in the street called to him, 'Only the Old Lord is at home. His servant may answer you, if she wants to. Call for her. Her name is Cuckoo.' And he laughed.

Wang Lung turned to the gates and knocked once more. The gates opened a little and a voice demanded, 'Who is it?'

'It is Wang Lung.'

'Who is this dog, Wang Lung?' the voice said rudely.

Wang Lung realized he was speaking to the Old Lord himself. Only a lord would speak in this rude way – a lord who had always given orders to servants.

'Sir,' Wang Lung said politely. 'I have come on business, I will not worry Your Lordship. May I speak with the agent who serves Your Honour?'

'That dog is gone,' said the Old Lord.

'I have come to talk about money,' continued Wang Lung.

Then the Old Lord pushed the gates closed. 'There is no money in this house.'

'But Sir,' called Wang Lung, 'I come to pay you money, not to take it from you.'

Then another voice cried out, 'That is something I have not heard in a long time.'

And a woman came to the gates and opened them. She had a narrow, sharp face, like a bird. She had painted her face so that she looked neither old nor young. Her voice was bitter and cruel. This was the servant Cuckoo.

'What is your business? Where is your money?' demanded the woman called Cuckoo.

'I cannot do business with a servant,' said Wang Lung.

'The Old Mistress is dead. The Old Lord is weak and ill,' said Cuckoo. 'Have you not heard about the bandits? They took everything. I am the only servant left in the House of Hwang. So, do business with me or do not do business with anyone.'

'Where are the Young Lords?' asked Wang Lung.

'Gone,' said the woman. 'Now, quickly, tell me what you want or go away.'

'How much land is there left?'

And immediately the woman understood what Wang Lung wanted. 'There is still much land. It is not all in one place, but it can all be sold.'

'Will the Old Lord agree to sell it?' asked Wang Lung.

'He will – he will,' the woman answered quickly. 'For he

does everything I say and he needs the money.'

Then Wang Lung asked, 'Will you sell the land for gold or for silver or for jewels?'

The woman answered quickly, 'I will sell it for jewels.'

8

Cuckoo, Lotus and the Tea-house[55]

Wang Lung was no longer a poor farmer with a few fields. He now owned a lot of land. He built another room onto his house and he hired men to work on his land. Also, he remembered the idle sons of the House of Hwang and decided his own sons would work on the land.

He took his small sons to the fields each day and told them to work with the ox as it pulled the plough. The boys' small hands could not do much work. But they learnt about the heat of the sun on their bodies. And they learnt about the tiredness that comes from walking up and down the fields.

Wang Lung did not let his wife work in the fields. He was no longer a poor man and O-lan stayed at home where she tended the house and made clothes.

Once more, O-lan was with child. This time she gave birth to twins – a boy and a girl.

Wang Lung thought, for the first time in his life, that he could not have any worries or sadness. But now his oldest daughter brought him sadness.

Five years passed, but his oldest girl did not speak. She

only smiled. She had come so near to death in the first year of her life, that she was left with no reason in her mind[56].

'My little fool – my poor little fool,' Wang Lung said again and again. 'You will never be married. But if I had sold this poor mouse to be a slave, they would have killed her when they found she was without reason.' And he cared for her and she followed him silently and smiled.

Another thing came to worry Wang Lung. He was ashamed that at the market he must say, 'Will you read this bill of sale to me, for I cannot read or write.'

So he took his two sons away from their work in the fields and took them to the school. An old schoolmaster taught boys for a small sum of money at each feast day.

'Sir,' said Wang Lung to the schoolmaster, 'these are my two idle sons. If you can make them learn anything, you will please me well.'

The old schoolmaster asked Wang Lung about his work and Wang Lung answered that he was a farmer. So the schoolmaster gave the boys names. He called the twelve-year-old boy Nung En and the eleven-year-old boy Nung Wen. The names meant 'wealth from the earth'.

As he left the schoolmaster's house, Wang Lung met a neighbour.

'I have just come from my sons' school,' he said proudly. 'I do not need the boys to work in the fields. They can learn to read and write instead.'

––––

So the prosperity of Wang Lung's house grew. And for seven years the rains came and the fields were green and there was neither hunger nor thirst. But, in the eighth year, the rains fell in the north without stopping. The river rose higher and higher and it flooded the fields, so that men could neither plant nor reap.

Wang Lung told his workmen to build and repair walls and to tend animals. He, himself was idle for the first time in his life and had the time to watch his family.

The twins laughed and played in the doorway. His old father slept, woke and slept in a corner. His poor, foolish daughter sat for hours and hours twisting a piece of cloth in her hands. O-lan cooked, mended clothes and tended the house.

O-lan's hair was now grey. Her body was tired from hard work and her teeth had become black.

'You look like the wife of a farmer,' said Wang Lung. 'Can you not put some sweet oil on your hair, as other women do? Can you not wear clothes like other women? You are the wife of a prosperous man.'

O-lan thought he was complaining that she had not given him more sons. And she answered, 'Since the twins were born, I have not been well. There is a fire in my belly.'

'Well, I shall go to the tea-house and hear the news,' said Wang Lung. And so he left and went into town.

Years ago, the people in the old tea-house had been rude to Wang Lung. But now, when he entered this tea-house, men spoke quietly to one another, 'That is Wang Lung – the one who bought the land from the House of Hwang.' At first, Wang Lung had been pleased but he was now tired of this. And so he went to a new tea-house where men did not know him.

This new tea-house had two floors. On the ground floor, men sat drinking tea and gambling with dice and dominoes[57]. They were very noisy. On the upper floor, there were women who entertained men. At night the singing of the women and their laughter came from the windows.

Wang Lung sat drinking his tea. There was noise all around him, so he did not hear footsteps behind him. But he turned when a woman's voice said, 'Wang Lung, the farmer. What are you doing here?'

He saw the sharp, narrow, handsome face of the Old Lord's servant called Cuckoo. And he answered loudly above the noise of gambling men, 'Is not my money as good as another man's? I am a wealthy man. I have had good fortune.'

'Everyone has heard of Wang Lung's good fortune,' said Cuckoo. 'Perhaps you wish to gamble with dice? Show us how good your fortune is.'

'I have never touched dice or wine,' said Wang Lung.

'Oh? You drink only tea?' Cuckoo looked at him with her head held sideways and her lips open in a wide smile. 'You say you have never gambled or drunk strong wine. But have you touched pretty hands and a sweet face?' And she laughed.

Wang Lung's face became red. 'No, I have not.'

'But you dream of them, do you not?' asked Cuckoo. Wang Lung was silent. Then Cuckoo took a painting from the pocket of her dress. On the painting were pictures of pretty women.

'Wang Lung, the farmer. What are you doing here?'

'Now, these are dream women,' said Cuckoo. 'These are the women that men visit in their dreams. Not you, of course. Other men. You are a good farmer with many sons. You do not need these painted women.'

And she saw how Wang Lung looked at the pictures and how his eyes became bright with the thought of the pretty women.

'Now, if ...,' continued Cuckoo, '... if you chose one of these women – but they are not real women – which one would you choose?'

And the blood ran in Wang Lung's body with the heat of fire. He looked at the picture of a young woman. Her body was as slender as a shoot of bamboo. Her face was like a clever kitten's face. Her hand held a lotus flower. Wang Lung did not speak but he stared at the picture.

Then he paid for his tea and went out quickly. The sound of Cuckoo's laughter followed him into the street.

9

Lotus Comes to Wang Lung's House

Water lay upon the fields and Wang Lung was idle. If there had been work to do, he might never have gone to the tea-house again. He would have forgotten the picture of the girl with the painted face and the body as slender as a shoot of bamboo. But he had no work and he was restless. He did not know what to do.

He walked up and down inside the house. At last, he went to the tea-house and saw Cuckoo standing in the doorway.

'Wang Lung, the farmer,' Cuckoo said in her sharp voice. 'What do you want?'

'If I have silver, may I not do as other men do?' said Wang Lung and he opened his hand and showed silver dollars to Cuckoo.

Cuckoo looked at the silver, then said, 'Come upstairs. Choose the woman you like.'

'The little one,' said Wang Lung. 'The one with the lotus flower in her hand.'

Cuckoo smiled and led him upstairs. A door opened and a woman looked at Wang Lung.

'The first man of the night,' she said.

'He is not for you,' Cuckoo said in her sharp and cruel voice. 'He has come to see Lotus.'

'Good,' said the other woman, 'for he smells like a farmer.'

Then Cuckoo opened a door and pushed Wang Lung into a room where a slender girl sat on a bed.

———

All the long summer, while the fields were covered in water, Wang Lung went to the tea-house each night. The good silver which he had earned was soon gone.

Each time he visited Lotus, she would sigh and say, 'Ah me – ah me.'

And he would ask, 'What is it, my little flower? Why are you sad?'

And Lotus would answer, 'I have no joy today because my friend received a present. Her lover gave her a gold pin for her hair and all I have is this old silver pin.'

So Wang Lung bought Lotus many presents. And all his silver ran through his fingers like water.

At last he went to O-lan, his wife, and said, 'Give me those two pearls which you kept. They are no use to you.'

And O-lan answered sadly, 'I thought one day I might have them made into earrings. I was going to give them to our youngest daughter on her marriage day.'

'Give them to me!' Wang Lung demanded.

So O-lan gave him the two pearls, which were her only possessions except the clothes on her back. She said nothing, but tears came into her eyes and she cried silently.

———

Then Wang Lung's uncle and his uncle's wife came to live with them. This uncle was the youngest brother of Wang Lung's father.

'Nephew, you are prosperous,' said Wang Lung's uncle. 'We have come to live with you because we are poor.'

Wang Lung did not answer. He knew his uncle was an idle man and his uncle's wife was a sharp-tongued woman. She also knew Cuckoo, and she knew all the gossip[58] of the town.

'Cuckoo is a clever woman,' said his uncle's wife. 'After the Old Lord died in her bed, she went to the new tea-house. And I hear you visit the new tea-house often.'

'What of it?' said Wang Lung.

'They say, in the town, that you will take a concubine into your house.'

Wang Lung had not thought of this, but he liked the idea of Lotus becoming his concubine. His eyes became bright and the woman saw his desire. But he would need a go-between[59] to make the arrangements.

'Can this thing be arranged?' he asked.

'Yes, I can arrange it,' said his uncle's wife.

'Then let it be done.'

And Wang Lung ordered his workmen to build more rooms onto the house. When she saw this O-lan asked, 'Why are you building more rooms?'

'Another woman is coming to this house,' answered Wang Lung.

Then O-lan cried, 'I have borne you sons! I have borne you sons!'

Soon his uncle's wife came to Wang Lung and said, 'The owner of the tea-house will release[60] Lotus if you pay a hundred silver dollars. And Lotus will come to live in your house if you give her jade earrings, a gold ring and two suits of clothes. And she will bring Cuckoo as her servant.'

Wang Lung did not listen to all this. He said, 'Let it be done. Let it be done.'

And he gave silver to his uncle's wife, saying, 'Keep ten dollars for yourself.'

'No, no,' said the woman. 'We are one family and I do this for you and not for silver.'

But she put out her hand as she said these words. And Wang Lung filled her hand with silver.

Then the arrangement was made and, on a sunny day at the end of summer, Lotus came to live in Wang Lung's house.

———

There was no peace in Wang Lung's house after he brought Lotus to live there. He thought O-lan would hate Lotus because he had heard this always happened when a second woman came to a house. But, no, O-lan did not hate Lotus. She hated Cuckoo with a great hate.

'I knew that one when I was in the House of Hwang,' said O-lan. 'Twenty times a day she came to the kitchen. She shouted orders. "Tea for the Lord! Food for the Lord!" And always it was too hot or too cold or badly prepared.'

So Wang Lung told his workmen to build another kitchen and an inner courtyard. Then there were two homes in Wang Lung's house.

Next, his old father broke the peace of the house. The old man was now very old. He slept and woke and slept and cared for nothing except his food. He could not understand why another kitchen had been built.

One day, he saw the doorway to the inner courtyard. Perhaps he could get more food there. He pulled open the curtain over the doorway and he saw Lotus standing in the inner courtyard beside a pool of fish. Her face was painted with red on her cheeks and black on her eyebrows.

'Harlot![61]' he cried in his high, trembling voice. 'There is a harlot in the house!'

Then Wang Lung led the old man quickly back to his own room. He was afraid that Lotus would be angry. For, if Lotus became angry, she screamed and beat her hands together and would not be comforted unless Wang Lung gave her an expensive gift.

On another day, he heard Lotus scream and he ran to her inner courtyard. There, he found that the young twins had taken their older sister – his poor fool – to visit Lotus.

'I cannot bear fools!' screamed Lotus. 'Take her away! Take her away! A fool brings bad fortune.'

Wang Lung was angry. Of all his children, the Poor Fool was his favourite. Lotus's screams had frightened his older daughter, so he said with great gentleness to the twins, 'My son and my daughter, take our poor fool back to her place in the sun.'

Then he turned to Lotus and said angrily, 'I will not hear my children cursed. Not by you – who has not borne a son and will never bear sons.'

Lotus was afraid, for now she knew he loved her less than before. 'I will obey my lord,' she said. And she stood with her head bowed. Wang Lung left Lotus and did not return to her inner courtyard for many days.

10

Wang Lung's Family

The flood waters dried up at last and left the land wet and green.

'Where is my hoe?' cried Wang Lung. 'Where is my plough? Where is the seed for planting?'

He led his men out into the fields and they worked all day in the hot sun. And so Wang Lung was happy again.

Wang Lung felt that there was peace in his house

'Take her away! Take her away!
A fool brings bad fortune.'

because he treated both his women well. O-lan pleased him because she was the mother of his sons. Lotus pleased him because she had a beautiful face and body.

The two older boys, Nung En and Nung Wen, were young men now and they were tired of school. Wang Lung knew that he must find employment for Nung En, the oldest son because he was clever and would not work in the fields. And O-lan said, 'You must find him a wife.'

So Wang Lung spoke to a merchant in the town. 'We have done business for many years. You have bought my corn. You have a daughter and my oldest son, Nung En, needs a wife.'

The merchant knew Wang Lung and understood what he was asking. It would be useful to marry his daughter to the son of a rich farmer. But the two men did not speak about the marriage at this time, they only agreed that such an arrangement was possible.

Wang Lung returned home and told Cuckoo to arrange the marriage. Immediately, Cuckoo thought of the money she would get. She quickly agreed to be the go-between. Then Wang Lung sent for Nung En to tell him about the marriage, but his oldest son could not be found.

'Where is he?' demanded Wang Lung. He questioned everyone in the house. But no one knew where the young man had gone.

Wang Lung told one of his men to wait at the gate of the house and to tell him when his son came home. But Nung En did not come back to the house until dawn. He staggered and vomited[62] in the courtyard and fell down and lay in his vomit.

O-lan ran out to help her son. She washed him and put him in his bed. Wang Lung saw that the young man was drunk and could not be questioned. So he went to Nung Wen, his second son and demanded, 'Where has your older brother been?' But the boy was silent. 'Tell me!' shouted Wang Lung.

The boy bowed his head and said, 'My older brother will beat me if I tell you.'

'Tell me what?' shouted Wang Lung. And he got hold of the boy by the throat and shook him.

'Nung En was with our cousin – your uncle's son,' said the boy who was very frightened.

Wang Lung threw the boy to the ground and went to the rooms of his uncle. There he found his uncle's son and saw that he was drunk too.

'What did you make my son do?' demanded Wang Lung.

'I did not make him do anything,' said the young man rudely.

Then Wang Lung got hold of him and said, 'Tell me or die.'

'He was at the old House of Hwang, where the harlot lives,' the young man answered.

Wang Lung knew about this harlot, because the whole town knew about her. She had been one of the Old Lord's concubines and a servant in the House of Hwang.

Then Wang Lung decided to send Nung En away and to order his uncle and his uncle's son to leave his house.

'Get out of my house,' he said to his uncle. 'I will burn the house rather than give you shelter.'

'You dare not order me to leave,' said his uncle. And he opened his robe to show a piece of red cloth.

Now this piece of red cloth was the sign of a group of bandits called the Redbeards who were much feared. They robbed people, burned their homes and carried away women from the villages. Suddenly Wang Lung realized why these bandits had never come to his house. His own uncle was a Redbeard!

Wang Lung knew what he had to do.

'Eat what you want in my house,' he said, though he was very angry. 'And I will give you some money to spend.'

So he left his uncle to eat and drink and never spoke about this again.

Then Cuckoo came back from the merchant and said, 'He has agreed to let your oldest son, Nung En, marry his daughter. But the girl is only fourteen years old. You must wait three more years before they can marry.'

Nung En was eighteen years old now and would no longer go to school in the town. He said, 'Let me go to the city in the south. I will not stay in this house and be watched like a child. And the town here is no bigger than a village.'

So Wang Lung gave the boy money and told him to go to the city in the south. The young man studied with new teachers and read many books and Wang Lung became proud that his son was a scholar.

———

When the young man was gone, Wang Lung looked at his family. O-lan sat sewing each day. His poor fool played with a piece of cloth. The second son, Nung Wen, was at

Suddenly Wang Lung realized why these bandits had never come to his house.

school and the twins were now almost ten years old. Lotus was more beautiful than when she was young.

He was pleased with his life. He decided it was time to arrange employment and marriage for two more of his children.

His oldest son, Nung En, was a big strong young man and looked like O-lan. But the second boy, Nung Wen, was small and had sharp intelligent eyes. He looked like Wang Lung's father. 'He will make a good merchant,' thought Wang Lung.

So he went to the merchant, who was to be father-in-law to his oldest son, and said, 'I want to apprentice[63] my second son, Nung Wen.'

The merchant answered, 'I have need of a clever young man.'

'That is good,' said Wang Lung.

'Also I have a son of ten years,' said the merchant. 'And you have a daughter of ten years. Shall we have two marriages together?'

Wang Lung quickly agreed to this and went home to tell his second son, 'You are going to be apprenticed to the merchant in town.' The boy was pleased that he was going to leave school.

Then Wang Lung told his second daughter, 'You will marry the merchant's son when you are old enough.'

Wang Lung looked at his daughter closely and saw there were tears on her face, 'Do not be sad,' he said. 'Why do you cry?'

'Because my mother binds my feet[64] every night,' answered the girl, 'so that I may get a good husband. And so that my husband may love me. For my mother does not have bound feet and says she is ugly and that you do not love her.'

Wang Lung was ashamed when he heard this. Had he not been a good husband? And had he not treated O-lan well? He looked at O-lan, who was tired and grey-haired although she was not old. He saw how slowly she moved and how she put her hand on her belly from time to time.

'Help your mother with her work,' he told his youngest daughter.

Months passed, but Wang Lung could not forget his daughter's words, 'My mother says you do not love her.'

One day, O-lan began to clear away their meal when her face became pale and covered with a sweat of pain.

'What is it?' Wang Lung asked sharply.

'It is the fire in my belly,' said O-lan. 'There is a swelling in my belly as hard as a rock.'

Then Wang Lung told his wife to lie down and do no work. He went into town to find a doctor.

The doctor had a long white beard and spectacles with metal frames. The sleeves of his robe covered his hands. Wang Lung described his wife's illness.

'I will come at once,' said the old doctor.

When they came to O-lan's bed, she had fallen asleep and there was sweat on her face. The doctor examined her and said, 'There is a great swelling in her belly, as hard as a rock.'

'Can you make her well?' asked Wang Lung.

'It is a difficult illness,' said the doctor. 'I can only give her herbs[65] for the pain.'

Then Wang Lung understood that O-lan was going to die. He thanked the doctor and paid him ten silver dollars. Then he stood alone in the kitchen where O-lan had spent so much of her life. And suddenly he cried.

11
The Death of O-lan

O-lan was not an old woman. Her body was strong and she lay for many months on her bed. She ate and drank only a little. Her body became thin and brown like an autumn leaf but her belly stayed swollen.

The merchant sent his daughter to Wang Lung's house. She was a kind girl of seventeen years and she looked after O-lan.

When O-lan saw the girl, she spoke, 'There is one thing I want before I die. I want to see my oldest son and this girl married.'

'Do not speak of dying,' said Wang Lung. But he sent a messenger to the city in the south. He asked Nung En to come home quickly.

And soon the oldest son came home. Wang Lung was pleased to see that his son was now a fine young man and he forgot the worry his son had given him.

The son went to his mother and comforted her, 'You look better than father told me. Surely you will get well?'

he said.

But O-lan answered, 'I will see you get married, then I will die.'

So Wang Lung arranged the marriage for the next day and invited many guests and brought cooks from the town. There was much feasting and happiness. Even the old man, Wang Lung's father, who was too old to understand, called out, 'A marriage! And a marriage means children!'

The bride and groom went to see O-lan. They sat by her bed and she watched them eat the marriage rice and drink the marriage wine. 'My son and my daughter,' she said, 'look after your father and your grandfather, and look after my poor fool.'

When the marriage feast was over, O-lan slept a while. Wang Lung sat by her bed while she woke and slept and woke.

'I am ugly, but I have borne sons,' said O-lan. 'I am a slave, but there are sons in my house.'

At last O-lan stared at Wang Lung as if she did not know him. Then her head fell back and she was dead.

Wang Lung made all the arrangements for O-lan's funeral. The whole family watched as O-lan's body was put into its coffin.

The old man, Wang Lung's father, saw O-lan put into her coffin and he cried. Then he went to his bed and lay down and died. And so the house of Wang Lung had two funerals together.

Everyone dressed in white clothes because white is the colour of death. They carried the two coffins to a hill on Wang Lung's land and there they buried Wang Lung's

They sat by her bed and she watched them eat the marriage rice and drink the marriage wine.

wife, O-lan, and his father. There were many tears and much crying. But although there was so much unhappiness, the Poor Fool, who had no reason, smiled and laughed.

————

Two of his family were now gone but the house of Wang Lung grew and grew. There were now his son, Nung En and his wife, his uncle and his wife, servants and workers. It was time for his second son, Nung Wen to marry and add to this number. Where would he put them all?

Wang Lung thought about this as he walked through the town and came to the empty house that was once the Great House of Hwang. The gates of wood and iron that were guarded by two stone lions were open. In the outer courtyards, a crowd of poor people had made huts from mats.

Wang Lung was now a rich landowner. He was no longer a poor farmer. He had land. He had silver and gold. He looked on the people in the outer courtyards and saw they were dirty and unwashed.

The doors of the inner courtyards of the Great House of Hwang were closed. A very old woman lived in the gate-keeper's house and Wang Lung recognized her. She was the wife of the gatekeeper who had led Wang Lung to see the Great Lady all those years ago.

'Wake up, woman, and show me the inner courtyards,' Wang Lung commanded.

'I can only show the courtyards to those who want to buy them or rent[66] them,' said the woman.

Then Wang Lung thought, 'I own all of the land of

75

the House of Hwang. Why should I not have the house as well?'

'Show the courtyards to me,' commanded Wang Lung. 'For I will have this house.'

———

Now, in these days, when Wang Lung decided something, he wished it to be done quickly. He grew angry if things were not done quickly. He arranged to rent the House of Hwang and wished his family to move there immediately.

But he stayed in his own house after the rest of his family had moved to the House of Hwang. Only Ching, his old foreman, and his poor fool stayed with him.

Wang Lung always kept his oldest daughter near him and he fed her and washed her himself. The rest of his family did nothing for her. His oldest son's wife said, 'Such a fool should not have been allowed to live.'

At last, he went to the House of Hwang. He lived there in his own courtyards with his poor fool who sat all day in the sun.

Still there was not peace in his house. His uncle's son and his oldest son argued. His uncle and his uncle's wife demanded more rooms and more food and more servants. Wang Lung did not know what to do with them all.

He went into a tobacco shop, because he now liked to smoke tobacco in a pipe at night. While the tobacconist was getting the tobacco, Wang Lung smelt a sweet smell coming from the back of the shop. The smell made him think of the Great Lady of the House of Hwang.

'Do you have opium as well as tobacco?' Wang Lung asked.

'It is not lawful to sell opium these days,' answered the tobacconist. 'But it is sold in the room behind the shop. The cost is a silver dollar for one ounce.'

'I will buy six ounces,' said Wang Lung.

That night he invited his uncle to smoke a pipe with him. And he said, 'I found this among my father's things.' He gave the opium to his uncle. 'I bought it when my father could not sleep. Do you wish to smoke it?'

His uncle's eyes became bright, 'I have smoked it, but opium is too expensive to smoke often.'

'There is more,' Wang Lung said. 'Perhaps your wife would like to smoke some?'

From that day, Wang Lung bought opium for his uncle and his uncle's wife and they were quiet. Then his cousin, who was wild and rough, said, 'There is a war in the south. I will go and fight.'

Wang Lung said to his uncle's wife, 'Your son will become a military officer. He will bring great merit to our family.' But, in his heart, he said, 'Many men are killed in wars. I hope he is one of them.'

Wang Lung hoped for peace in his house now. But his oldest son's wife gave birth to a son. And his oldest son said to him, 'We are now a great family. Let us buy all of the house that was Hwang's. Let it be the House of Wang Lung.'

So Wang Lung gave his oldest son money to buy the house because money came easily to Wang Lung from all his lands. Now Wang Lung hoped for peace. But then his second son came and said, 'Why are you spending all this money? If we lent[67] the money at twenty per cent interest, it would come back to us five times over.'

Wang Lung saw that these two sons would always argue about money. But his third son worked on the land and Wang Lung was pleased with this boy.

But then the third son came to him and said, 'Am I to work on the land and be ignorant? My brothers laugh at me because I cannot read and write. Send me to a school in the south or find me a teacher.'

So Wang Lung found a teacher for his third son because he wanted no more arguments. All he wanted was peace. He was growing older. He wished only to enjoy the wealth he had made.

But his oldest son always worried that the house was not fine enough. And the second son always worried that the family spent too much money. And his third son was angry that he had not gone to school when he was young.

His older daughter – the Poor Fool – gave him pleasure. She wanted nothing. She sat in the sun and played with her piece of cloth and smiled. Also his oldest grandson gave him pleasure. The boy ran around the many court-yards of the Great House of Wang Lung. These courtyards were neither great nor small to the boy, for he had known no other home.

12

War Comes to the North

One last problem came for Wang Lung. The war came to the town and with it came a group of soldiers. These soldiers were no better than bandits and their leader was the son of Wang Lung's uncle.

Wang Lung's cousin was a big, rough man, and when he walked into the House of Wang Lung, he demanded, 'Where is my mother?'

So Wang Lung took him to his mother. The woman had been smoking opium for many years. She was now an ill woman whose skin was yellow.

'What have you done to her?' demanded his uncle's son.

Wang Lung answered, 'Cousin, she is old. Let her do what she wishes.'

Then the soldiers stayed in the courtyards of Wang Lung. They broke the furniture and made the pools and the beds dirty. They drank wine and shouted and sent for women.

The leader of the soldiers – Wang Lung's cousin – saw a young girl called Pear Blossom who was Lotus's servant.

'Bring the girl to my bed,' he demanded.

Pear Blossom was small and slender. Wang Lung had bought her as a slave and had treated her well. The poor girl cried and ran to Wang Lung.

Lotus was angry and shouted at Pear Blossom, 'Go to

the leader of the soldiers. He is a man and all men are the same. Go to his bed. If you do not the soldiers will destroy this house.'

But the girl cried and Wang Lung was kind to her. 'Find another girl,' he said to Lotus and Cuckoo. 'Pear Blossom is too young.'

And a servant girl, who was much older and fully grown, said, 'I will go to the soldier.'

So Wang Lung's cousin took the servant girl to his bed. Meanwhile, Pear Blossom stayed with Wang Lung because she feared the anger of Lotus.

———

The soldiers went away at last to fight in the war. Before they went, their leader shouted to Wang Lung, 'Cousin, I have made a child, a grandson for my mother.' Then he was gone and Wang Lung started to repair the house.

The servant girl gave birth to a daughter. Wang Lung treated her well. He found a husband for her – a poor farmer. She married the farmer as O-lan had married Wang Lung. And Wang Lung sat in the hall, where the Old One of the House of Hwang had sat. And the farmer and the servant girl stood in front of him.

'Obey this man, your husband,' he commanded. 'Bear him sons and more sons.' And so the two were married.

After a time, Wang Lung's youngest son came to him and said, 'Father, I want the slave girl called Pear Blossom.'

Then Wang Lung felt jealous[68]. He had kept Pear Blossom in his courtyards and she cared for his poor fool of a daughter. He would not answer his son and his son became angry.

Pear Blossom was afraid. She came to Wang Lung and looked at him. Wang Lung felt heat in his blood and looked at her with desire. And Pear Blossom fell into his arms.

But Wang Lung pushed her away from him, saying, 'I am an old man. A young girl should have a young man.'

Pear Blossom answered, 'I like old men. Old men are kind. Young men are fierce.'

So Pear Blossom became Wang Lung's concubine and she comforted him in his old age. She cared for him and for his poor fool.

At first, Lotus was angry that Pear Blossom had taken her place. But, Wang Lung sent her gifts and food and she was happy. Lotus was now old and fat and was pleased that Wang Lung no longer came to her bed.

The youngest son was angry that his father had taken the slave he desired. 'I will become a soldier,' he said and left the house. Where he went, no one knew.

13

The House of Wang Lung

Wang Lung's life passed from autumn into winter. His desire for Pear Blossom changed as he grew older. Now she became his companion, not his concubine.

He had thought many times of who would look after his poor fool.

'When I am dead, no one will feed her,' he told Pear

Blossom. So he bought a little packet of white poison from the medicine shop, and he said to Pear Blossom, 'This poison is a gate of peace[69] for my poor fool. When I am dead, mix this with her rice and she will follow me.'

But Pear Blossom would not take the packet from him, 'I cannot kill your daughter,' she said. 'How can I kill her? I will care for her. I will take this poor fool and look after her.' look after her.'

Then Wang Lung said, 'Why do you do this for me?'

And Pear Blossom answered, 'You have been kind to me – kinder than any man in all my life.'

And so old age came to Wang Lung. He slept in the sun and woke and slept, as his old father had done.

He forgot the number of his grandchildren. 'Eleven grandsons and eight granddaughters,' they told him. And he laughed, 'Do I have that many?' And he forgot and he would ask them again.

He spoke to his grandchildren in a kind voice, 'Do you go to school?'

'Yes, grandfather,' they answered together.

'Do you study the Four Books[70]?'

The grandchildren laughed. 'There has been a Revolution. No one studies the Four Books since the Revolution.'

'I have heard of this thing,' said Wang Lung. 'I am told my youngest son, your uncle, is an official in this Revolution.'

At last Wang Lung knew that he was going to die soon and he spoke to his oldest son, 'I shall return to the earth house, where I was born. When I have seen it, and when I have looked on the place where your mother lies, I shall die. Bury me beside her.'

'Do not speak of your death,' said the oldest son. 'But I shall do as you ask.'

So Wang Lung returned to the earth house where he was born. His sons walked behind him and Pear Blossom held his hand.

They went to the small hill where his father and O-lan were buried. He saw where he would be buried and he said, 'I am happy.'

Then he said he wished to lie down in the earth house on the bed where O-lan had died.

As they all walked slowly back to the earth house, Wang Lung's sons talked as though their father were not there.

'We will sell this field. We will send our rice on the new railroad to the cities by the sea.'

Wang Lung stopped and picked up a handful of the good earth. 'If you sell the land, my sons, it is the end.'

Then they smiled at him, saying, 'We will never sell the land, father.'

And they led him to his bed in the earth house, but, above their old father's head they looked at each other and smiled.

'If you sell the land, my sons, it is the end.'

Points for Understanding

1

1 Where do Wang Lung and his father live?
2 What does Wang Lung's old father complain about?
3 Write a list of the things Wang Lung does before he goes to the town?
4 Why had Wang Lung's father visited the House of Hwang?
5 What is Wang Lung going to buy in the town?
6 Why does Wang Lung become angry with the barber?
7 Describe these people
  (a) the gatekeeper (b) the Great Lady (c) O-lan
8 Why is Wang Lung pleased with his new wife?

2

1 How does O-lan help her husband?
2 Why does Wang Lung give O-lan money for a red coat?
3 How do you know that Wang Lung is pleased to have a son?

3

1 'Wang Lung, the farmer,' said the gatekeeper. 'You have had good fortune.'
  Why is the gatekeeper polite to Wang Lung?
2 What does Wang Lung buy with his silver?

4

1 Before winter O-lan gave birth to another child. How many children does Wang Lung have now?
2 Why do Wang Lung and his family have to leave their land?
3 Why is Wang Lung pleased that he has land and not silver?
4 Where does Wang Lung's family decide to go?
5 How are they going to travel?

5

1 Where do Wang Lung and his family live in the city?
2 What happens at the public kitchens?
3 How do O-lan and the children get money?
4 How does Wang Lung get money?
5 Why does Wang Lung beat his younger son?

6

1 Why doesn't Wang Lung go back to his own land?
2 What does O-lan say they could do with Wang Lung's daughter?
  What is Wang Lung's reply?
3 Wang Lung listens to his neighbour and hears a group of men
  speaking in the city. What does he learn about the rich and the
  poor?
4 'We must go back to our land,' Wang Lung says to O-lan.
  Why does he say this?
5 What happens inside the Great House after the enemy breaks the
  gates of the city?

7

1 Who is Ching?
2 Where did O-lan get the jewels from?
3 Why does she want to keep two pearls?
4 Why does Wang Lung go to the House of Hwang? What happens
  there?

8

1 'My poor little fool.'
  Who is Wang Lung talking about? Why does he call this person
  this name?
2 Why does Wang Lung decide to send his two older sons to school?
3 How long has O-lan been ill?
4 Who does Wang Lung meet at the new tea-house?
5 Why does she laugh at Wang Lung?

9

1 Wang Lung asks O-lan for the pearls. Why does he do this?
2 Who comes to live in Wang Lung's house?
3 Which of these people does O-lan hate?
4 Why does Wang Lung become angry with Lotus?

10

1 Why does Wang Lung go to talk to the merchant in the town?
2 Why can Wang Lung not make his Uncle and his Uncle's son leave the house?
3 Why does Nung En go to the city in the south?
4 'Shall we have two marriages together?' asks the merchant. Whose marriages is the merchant talking about?
5 What does Wang Lung's second daughter say to make him ashamed?
6 The doctor examines O-lan. What does Wang Lung learn about his wife's illness?

11

1 Who looks after O-lan while she is ill?
2 Everyone dressed in white clothes because white is the colour of death. Who has died and where are they buried?
3 Wang Lung's family is now very large. What does he decide to do?
4 There was no peace in Wang Lung's house.
  (a) Why do Wang Lung's two older sons argue?
  (b) Why is his third son unhappy?
5 Which relations please Wang Lung? Why?

12

1 Who comes to live in the House of Wang Lung?
2 Who is Pear Blossom?
3 Why do Wang Lung and his youngest son argue about Pear Blossom.
4 What does Wang Lung do for the servant girl?

13

1 Why does Wang Lung give a packet of poison to Pear Blossom?
2 Pear Blossom would not take the packet of poison from Wang Lung. Why?
3 Why does Wang Lung want to return to the earth house?
4 How does he feel when he sees where his father and O-lan are buried?
5 Why is the land so important to Wang Lung? Why don't his sons understand this?
6 What do you think the sons will do with the land after their father is dead?

Glossary

1   *coughed – to cough* (page 12)
    a noise you make when your throat and mouth are dry.

2   *boil – to boil* (page 13)
    heat a liquid until bubbles come to the top and steam is made.

3   *complain – to complain* (page 13)
    speak in a way that shows you are unhappy about something or
    someone.

4   *comforted – to be comforted* (page 13)
    no longer worried by pain, unhappiness or fear.

5   *ashamed – to be ashamed* (page 15)
    feel unhappy about something you have thought or the way you
    have behaved.

6   *braided – to braid* (page 15)
    hair that is twisted together into a tail.
        For many years, men in China shaved the hair off their faces and
    the fronts of their heads. They left the hair at the backs of their
    heads to grow very long. They braided this hair into a long tail that
    hung down their backs. At the time of this story, men in the cities
    were not wearing braids. They were cutting their hair short in the
    European way.

7   *ground corn* (page 15)
    maize or wheat that has been crushed – ground – into flour.

8   *chopsticks* (page 15)
    two thin sticks used to carry food to the mouth.

9   *water chestnuts and bamboo shoots* (page 16)
    vegetables used in Chinese cooking. Water chestnuts come from
    plants that grow in rivers, lakes or ponds. Bamboo shoots are the
    soft new leaves of bamboo – tall plants with hard, round stems.

10 *soy-bean sauce* (page 16)
    a dark-brown sauce made from soya-beans.

11 *stick of incense* (page 16)
    incense is made from the seeds, stems and the dried juice of special
    plants. It has a strong smell when it burns. Incense is often made
    into long, thin sticks and burnt in temples to show respect to the
    gods.

12 *tend the house and work the fields and bear children* (page 16)
peasant women in China at this time had to work very, very hard.
They also had to work with their husbands in the fields. Chinese
women had to give birth to – bear – many children. If a man had
many children he had respect from other men and the children
could work with him.

13 *pock-marked* – *to be pock-marked* (page 16)
skin that is rough and marked by a disease.

14 *split upper lip* (page 16)
sometimes babies were born with a hole in their top lip. People
thought that this happened because families were poor or ill.

15 *ignorance* (page 17)
Wang Lung doesn't know about life in the town. He understands
that the barbers think he is stupid and slow because he is a poor
farmer.

16 *squares of bean-curd* (page 17)
a food used in Chinese cooking. Soya-beans are ground and then
mixed with water and cooked. This mixture is then pressed so that
it looks like pieces of cheese.

17 *bride* (page 18)
a woman who is going to be married. A *bridegroom* is a man who is
going to be married. In China, men could have only one wife but
they could also have lovers – *concubines*. Concubines lived with a
man but were not married to them. The children of concubines had
to look after a man's wife and her children.

18 *guarded* – *to guard* (page 18)
look after someone's property. Lions carved from stone were often
put outside Chinese homes to stop evil spirits entering.

19 *demanded* – *to demand* (page 18)
ask for something or for information in a loud voice.

20 *expected* – *to be expected* (page 18)
the people in the house knew that Wang Lung was coming.

21 *courtyards* (page 19)
open areas inside the large house of a rich man. Courtyards often
had trees, flowers and ponds and were pleasant places to sit.

22 *pipe of opium* (page 19)
opium is a drug made from the seeds of poppy flowers. It is smoked
in a pipe and makes you feel very calm and peaceful. People used to
smoke opium so that they forgot their troubles or pain. Soon they
only wanted more and more of this dangerous drug. They did not
eat, work or care about anything.

23 **commanded** – *to command* (page 19)
speak in a strong way so that someone will do what you want.
24 **obey** – *to obey* (page 20)
do what you are told without asking questions.
25 **possessions** (page 22)
the few things that O-lan owns. For example, a few clothes, shoes, a hair comb.
26 **borne many hardships** – *to bear many hardships* (page 22)
live a life which is tiring and difficult. But see Glossary No. 12 – this does not mean to give birth to children.
27 **modest** (page 22)
someone who is quiet and does not think or talk about themselves.
28 **ox** (page 23)
a bull used for work on the farm.
29 **hoed** – *to hoe* (page 23)
dig the land using a metal hook on a wooden pole.
30 **reaped** – *to reap* (page 23)
cut the crops that have grown up and made seeds using a long knife.
31 **with pleasure** (page 23)
show happiness and joy when you look at someone or something.
32 **we will have a good harvest this year** (page 23)
Wang Lung's father is thinking that the family will have grown a child as well as food this year.
33 **ploughed** – *to plough* (page 24)
cut and turn over the earth using a metal blade pulled by the ox.
34 **sweat** (page 25)
water that comes out of your skin when you are hot, afraid or in pain.
35 **freshly peeled reed** (page 25)
reeds are long thin plants that grow in water. Wang Lung is going to take the leaves off the reed. The sharp stem will be used to cut the birth cord of the baby.
36 **quilt** (page 27)
a cover made of thick cotton that keeps you warm when you are sleeping.
37 **salted** – *to salt* (page 27)
meat that is covered with salt and dried. Salted meat can be kept for a long time.

38 **their secret treasure and comfort** (page 28)
O-lan hides the money in the wall of the farmhouse. It will be used by Wang Lung when he has to buy something important in the future.

39 **prospered** – *to prosper* (page 28)
had good fortune and success. O-lan had been an unhappy slave. Now she has food, a home and a family.

40 **sign of good fortune** (page 28)
boy babies were very important in China. Boys could help with the work and brought respect. It was very good luck if the first child was a boy.

41 **dare not** – *to dare not* (page 30)
not want to do something because you are afraid of someone or something.

42 **oily** (page 30)
a word meaning full of fat or grease. The agent speaks in a smooth, unpleasant way. He wants to make Wang Lung think that he is an important man in the House of Hwang.

43 **envy** – *to envy* (page 30)
a feeling of anger and hate because someone has got something that you want.

44 **trembling** – *to tremble* (page 32)
shaking with fear.

45 **A thousand curses** (page 33)
a way of wishing bad luck to someone.

46 **public kitchens** (page 36)
places where poor people could get food for very little money.

47 **get merit in heaven** (page 37)
Chinese people believed that if they did good deeds on earth when they were alive they would have good things in heaven when they died.

48 **laughed with embarrassment** – *to laugh with embarrassment* (page 38)
laugh because you are ashamed or uncomfortable about something.

49 **hired** – *to hire* (page 38)
pay money to someone to use something they have. Passengers paid the men who pulled the rickshaws to take them where they wanted to go. The men who pulled the rickshaws then gave some of this money to the owner of the rickshaws.

50 **stinking manure** (page 40)
   faeces, or dung, from animals. Wang Lung is surprised that the farmers put this strong smelling manure on their fields.
51 **oppress** – *to oppress* (page 44)
   a cruel and unfair way of making people do things.
52 **inner courtyard** (page 47)
   the most important courtyard in the centre of a large house. Outer courtyards were smaller areas inside a big house.
53 **bandits** (page 50)
   thieves.
54 **wealth** (page 50)
   valuable things such as money, gold or jewels.
55 **tea-house** (page 54)
   a place where Chinese men could go to drink tea or alcohol. Also they could win money by gambling and they could meet prostitutes.
56 **no reason in her mind** (page 55)
   Wang Lung's daughter has no intelligence. She cannot read, write, speak or look after herself.
57 **dice and dominoes** (page 57)
   dice are small cubes made of wood with numbers of dots painted on them. Dominoes are small, flat pieces of wood with dots painted on them. Games are played with dice or dominoes. You can gamble by guessing which number will come next.
58 **gossip** (page 61)
   unkind talk about other people.
59 **go-between** (page 62)
   someone who talks to the two people and tells each of them the other person's questions and answers.
60 **release** – *to release* (page 62)
   let someone go free if a payment is made. The tea-house owner bought the women who work there when they were young girls. Lotus cannot leave the tea-house unless Wang Lung buys her from the owner of the tea-house.
61 **Harlot!** (page 63)
   an insulting word meaning a prostitute.
62 **staggered and vomited** – *to stagger and vomit* (page 66)
   unable to walk properly and then to bring food up from your stomach through your mouth. Nung En is very ill from drinking alcohol – he is drunk.

63 **apprentice** – *to apprentice* (page 70)
pay someone to teach a young person to do a job. Wang Lung is going to pay the merchant to teach Nung Wen all about his business.

64 **binds my feet** – *to bind feet* (page 70)
tie cloth very tightly around the feet to keep them small. Until 1902, the daughters of rich Chinese families had their toes bent over and their feet bound when they were young. Chinese men thought women with bound feet were very attractive. These women were not able to work or to walk far from their homes. A wife with bound feet showed that a man was wealthy and important.

65 **herbs** (page 72)
plants whose leaves and seeds are used as medicine.

66 **rent** – *to rent* (page 75)
pay money to live in someone's house.

67 **lent** – *to lend* (page 77)
give someone money which they will have to pay back, at an extra charge, in the future.

68 **jealous** (page 80)
angry feelings because someone wants something you believe is yours.

69 **gate of peace** (page 82)
Wang Lung is worried that no-one will look after his poor fool when he is dead. He gives Pear Blossom poison to kill his oldest daughter. The words 'gate of peace' mean that when she is given the poison his daughter would sleep peacefully, die and then go into heaven.

70 **Four Books** (page 82)
the collection of the words of the philosopher Kung-fu-tzu (Confucius 551–479 BC).

INTERMEDIATE LEVEL

Oliver Twist *by Charles Dickens*
The Bonetti Inheritance *by Richard Prescott*
No Comebacks *by Frederick Forsyth*
The Enchanted April *by Elizabeth von Arnim*
The Three Strangers *by Thomas Hardy*
The Smuggler *by Piers Plowright*
The Pearl *by John Steinbeck*
The Woman Who Disappeared *by Philip Prowse*
A Town Like Alice *by Nevil Shute*
The Queen of Death *by John Milne*
Meet Me in Istanbul *by Richard Chisholm*
The Great Gatsby *by F. Scott Fitzgerald*
The Space Invaders *by Geoffrey Matthews*
My Cousin Rachel *by Daphne du Maurier*
I'm the King of the Castle *by Susan Hill*
Dracula *by Bram Stoker*
The Speckled Band and Other Stories *by Sir Arthur Conan Doyle*
The Queen of Spades and Other Stories *by Aleksandr Pushkin*
The Diamond Hunters *by Wilbur Smith*
When Rain Clouds Gather *by Bessie Head*
Banker *by Dick Francis*
No Longer at Ease *by Chinua Achebe*
The Franchise Affair *by Josephine Tey*
The Case of the Lonely Lady *by John Milne*
Silas Marner *by George Eliot*
Pride and Prejudice *by Jane Austen*
Wuthering Heights *by Emily Bronte*
Jurassic Park *by Michael Crichton*

For further information on the full selection of
Readers at all five levels in the series, please refer
to the Heinemann Readers catalogue.

Heinemann English Language Teaching
Halley Court, Jordan Hill, Oxford OX2 8EJ
A division of Reed Educational & Professional Publishing Limited

OXFORD MADRID FLORENCE ATHENS PRAGUE
SÃO PAULO MEXICO CITY CHICAGO PORTSMOUTH(NH)
TOKYO SINGAPORE KUALA LUMPUR MELBOURNE
AUCKLAND JOHANNESBURG IBADAN GABORONE

Heinemann is a registered trademark of Reed Educational & Professional
Publishing Limited

ISBN 0 435 27350 7

Illustrated by Mark Duffin
Typography by Adrian Hodgkins
Designed by Sue Vaudin
Cover by David Holmes and Marketplace Design
Typeset in 11.5/14.5 Goudy
Printed and bound in Malta by Interprint Limited

97 98 99 00 01 10 9 8 7 6 5 4 3 2